$17.95

05-07-15

Coaches

by Rebecca Pettiford

Ideas for Parents and Teachers

Bullfrog Books let children practice reading informational text at the earliest reading levels. Repetition, familiar words, and photo labels support early readers.

Before Reading

• Discuss the cover photo. Who might this book be about?

• Look at the picture glossary together. Read and discuss the words.

Read the Book

• "Walk" through the book and look at the photos. Let the child ask questions. Point out the photo labels.

• Read the book to the child, or have him or her read independently.

After Reading

• Prompt the child to think more. Ask: Have you had a coach teach you how to play a sport? What things did you learn from your coach?

Bullfrog Books are published by Jump!
5357 Penn Avenue South
Minneapolis, MN 55419
www.jumplibrary.com

Library of Congress Cataloging-in-Publication Data

Pettiford, Rebecca.
  Coaches / by Rebecca Pettiford.
    pages cm. — (Community helpers)
  Includes index.
  Audience: Age: 5.
  Audience: Grade: K to Grade 3.
  ISBN 978-1-62031-155-4 (hardcover) —
  ISBN 978-1-62496-242-4 (ebook)
  1. Coaches (Athletics)-—Juvenile literature.
  I. Title.
  GV711.P44 2015
  796.07'7—dc23
                                         2014032088

Series Editor: Wendy Dieker
Series Designer: Ellen Huber
Book Designer: Anna Peterson
Photo Researcher: Casie Cook

Photo Credits: All photos by Shutterstock except: Corbis, 4, 17, 22, 23tr; Dreamstime, cover, 16, 23tl; iStock, 8–9, 10–11, 13, 14–15, 23ml, 23bl; muzsy/Shutterstock, 21; SuperStock, 6–7, 23mr; Thinkstock, 1, 18–19.

Printed in the United States of America at Corporate Graphics in North Mankato, Minnesota.

Table of Contents

Coaches at Work

Jo wants to
be a coach.

What do they do?

They teach us how
to play a sport.

They teach
us teamwork.

They cheer us on!

Dan shows us soccer drills.

We pass the ball.

We run around cones.

He uses a stopwatch.

He times us.

stopwatch

Mia is in the gym.
Her coach helps her
on the mat.

Tweet! Bill blows a whistle.

We stop.

We listen.

13

Oh no!

Jed hurt his leg.

His coach makes
sure he's okay.

It's game day.
Ann has a clipboard.

She shows us plays.

They will help our team.

The other
team wins!

We are happy
for them.

We did our best.

Thanks for helping us, Coach!

On the Practice Field

whistle
Coaches blow a whistle to get the players' attention.

cones
Coaches use cones to mark where players should practice.

field
An outdoor space where a sport, such as soccer or football, is played.

Picture Glossary

clipboard
A small, thin board coaches use to hold paper and a pen.

plays
A coach's plan for winning a game; usually written on paper attached to a clipboard.

drills
A skill, such as passing a ball, that is practiced over and over again.

sport
A game in which players compete in certain activities and follow set rules.

gym
A room where indoor sports are played.

stopwatch
A watch with buttons that coaches use to time practice drills.

Index

To Learn More

Learning more is as easy as 1, 2, 3.

1) Go to www.factsurfer.com

2) Enter "coaches" into the search box.

3) Click the "Surf" button to see a list of websites.

With factsurfer.com, finding more information is just a click away.